Legends of Women's Tennis

By Martha London

Book design by Sarah Taplin
Cover design by Sarah Taplin

Photographs ©: Charles Krupa/AP Images, cover (left), 1 (left); Peter Morgan/AP Images, cover (right), 1 (right), 18; Andres Kudacki/AP Images, 4; Keystone-France/Gamma-Keystone/Getty Images, 7; PA Images/Getty Images, 9; AP Images, 10, 12; Marty Lederhandler/AP Images, 15; Robert Dear/AP Images, 17; NewsBase/AP Images, 21; Adam Butler/AP Images, 22; Lionel Cironneau/AP Images, 25; John Cordes/Icon Sportswire/AP Images, 26; Alastair Grant/AP Images, 29

Press Box Books, an imprint of Press Room Editions.

ISBN
978-1-63494-286-7 (library bound)
978-1-63494-304-8 (paperback)
978-1-63494-340-6 (epub)
978-1-63494-322-2 (hosted ebook)

Library of Congress Control Number: 2020913872

Distributed by North Star Editions, Inc.
2297 Waters Drive
Mendota Heights, MN 55120
www.northstareditions.com

Printed in the United States of America
012021

About the Author

Martha London works full-time writing children's books. When she isn't writing, you can find her hiking in the woods.

TABLE OF CONTENTS

adidas
NISSIN

CHAPTER 1

EARLY STARS

The crowd in Arthur Ashe Stadium roared. The veteran and legend Serena Williams was in the 2018 US Open finals. But Naomi Osaka, the 20-year-old upstart from Japan, was not about to be bowled over.

Osaka's 120-mile-per-hour (193-km/h) serve was difficult to return, even for the powerhouse Williams. Point by point and game by game, Osaka battled. The young star placed her shots deep in the court, keeping Williams on the run. She moved

Naomi Osaka reacts to winning a point during the 2018 US Open finals.

the champion from corner to corner, never allowing her a break.

At match point, Osaka took a deep breath. She appeared as calm as she'd been at the beginning of the match. She tossed the ball in the air. Her explosive serve carried deep into the corner of the service box. Williams couldn't return it. Osaka had just beaten her hero in straight sets to win the US Open.

Tennis did not always feature such diversity among its competitors. For many years, it was a sport for white people. Most players were upper-class too. Proper attire and proper etiquette were among the most important elements of the sport. But one of the most popular early stars wasn't considered proper

Suzanne Lenglen was far ahead of her time.

at all. Suzanne Lenglen was from France. At Wimbledon in 1919, she crashed her way through opponents to the title.

Lenglen was unlike any player at the time. She had flair, whereas other players were reserved. She leaped across the court as she dashed to get to balls. She bragged loudly after each point. People said she was rude.

But nobody could deny Lenglen's talent. She won that Wimbledon tournament. And over the next 10 years, she went on a winning streak few would top. She won five more Wimbledon titles and six French Open titles.

After Lenglen's reign, a new queen of the court emerged. Her name was Helen Wills Moody. The two could not have been more different. Moody was quiet and kept her emotions in check. The American nicknamed

Helen Wills Moody dominated the sport in the 1920s.

"Little Miss Poker Face" never let her opponent know what she was thinking. Her powerful serve and overhead helped her stay in control.

In seven years, she did not lose a set in singles. Her power and control earned her 19 Grand Slam singles titles. She also won two gold medals at the 1924 Olympics.

Nobody won more Grand Slam singles titles than Margaret Court. The aggressive Aussie won 24 of them in the 1960s and 1970s. She was especially dominant on her home court. She won the Australian Open 11 times.

ALTHEA GIBSON

Althea Gibson was tall and lanky. But she was strong. The American star made history in 1951 as the first Black woman invited to play at Wimbledon. Gibson didn't stop there, though. Her aggressive style of play helped her win championships around the world. In 1956, Gibson made history again. She was the first Black player to win a Grand Slam tournament when she beat top-seeded Angela Mortimer in the finals of the French Open. She went on to win Wimbledon and the US Open in each of the next two years.

Althea Gibson broke the color barrier in women's tennis.

CHAPTER 2

GROWING THE GAME

Billie Jean King wasn't afraid to attack the net. Quick and strong, she left her opponents no time to react to her powerful volleys. King won 12 Grand Slam singles titles between 1966 and 1975.

But King's most famous match wasn't part of any tournament. It was known as the "Battle of the Sexes." In 1973, King faced off against Bobby Riggs, a 55-year-old retired men's player. He loudly boasted that women could not be as good as men in tennis. So he challenged King,

Billie Jean King used her elite athletic ability to dominate her opponents.

the top women's player in the world, to a match to prove his point.

But King was too fast. Riggs could barely get a shot past her. Meanwhile, King kept Riggs on the run. He was never able to get into a rhythm. King won in three straight sets and took home the $100,000 prize. But King didn't stop there. She continued to be an influential advocate for equality in sports.

What King did to Riggs that day is what Chris Evert did to just about everyone on a clay surface. Most courts are made of asphalt. Clay courts make it a whole different game. Clay makes the ball bounce slower. But that was the way Evert liked it. She controlled points, directing her shots deep in the court.

Chris Evert took the tennis world by storm as a 16-year-old in 1971.

Matches against Evert became a matter of endurance. Evert almost always came out on top. Between 1973 and 1979, she went on a 125-match clay court winning streak. Through 2020, no one had topped that. Evert collected 18 Grand Slam singles titles in the 1970s and 1980s. A record seven titles came on the clay courts of the French Open.

While Evert dominated on clay, Martina Navratilova was queen of the grass. For several years, she and Evert were pinned as rivals, battling it out on Wimbledon's grass courts.

Navratilova was a serve-and-volley player. She was quick on her feet. After pounding her serves deep, she liked to race to the net. This tactic often allowed her to finish

Martina Navratilova made Wimbledon her own personal showcase in the 1980s.

DHL

points quickly by burying an opponent's weak return. From the late 1970s through the early 1990s, Navratilova racked up 18 Grand Slam singles titles. That included a record nine wins at Wimbledon.

Steffi Graf helped lead women's tennis to new heights in the 1980s and 1990s. The stoic German won all four Grand Slam tournaments in 1988. Not only was she still just 19 years old, she was only the third woman in history to do that in a single year. She followed her four Grand Slams with a gold medal at the Olympic Games. But Graf wasn't going to stop there. She continued to use her powerful forehand to crush the competition. Graf retired having won 22 Grand Slam singles titles.

Steffi Graf made history with her "Steffi Slam" in 1988.

At the 1990 Italian Open final, a little-known 16-year-old named Monica Seles crushed Navratilova 6–1, 6–1. Seles was only getting started. A month later, she beat Graf at the French Open. Tennis had a new star. Seles used two hands on both her forehand and backhand. She never sacrificed accuracy for power. Seles rarely made mistakes on the court.

She was on track to become one of the greatest tennis players of all time. But in 1993, a spectator rushed onto the court and stabbed her in the back. Seles eventually recovered and won another Grand Slam title in 1996. She followed that win with a bronze medal at the 2000 Olympics.

Monica Seles had an incredible run of success before her career was interrupted by an on-court attack.

Matrix

Reebok

CHAPTER 3

TO THE NEXT LEVEL

In the 2000s, players continued to get stronger. Tennis was not only a game of precision, but one of power. Serena and Venus Williams exemplified that.

The Williams sisters grew up in Compton, California. Trained by their father, the young Black women became huge stars in the mostly white, upper-class sport.

Early on, the sisters' careers paralleled one another. Then Serena began to pull ahead. In 2002, the sisters faced off at

The Williams sisters changed the game with their strength and charisma.

POWERFUL DUO

The Williams sisters don't always compete against one another. They are also a successful doubles team. Growing up together they learned how the other played. That, combined with their skills, often helped them make quick work of their opponents. As a doubles team, the sisters had won 14 Grand Slam titles and three Olympic gold medals through 2020.

the finals of the French Open, Wimbledon, and the US Open. Serena's powerful strokes outmatched those of her older sister, and she won all three titles. Serena continued to collect titles and accolades. By 2020, she had 23 Grand Slam titles, second only to Margaret Court.

Justine Henin won seven Grand Slam singles titles in the mid-2000s. The Belgian wielded a powerful serve and a one-handed backhand. But Henin did not just hit the ball hard. She was also

Justine Henin won her first Grand Slam title at the 2003 French Open.

INTERNATIONAUX DE FRANCE
SIMPLE DAMES
COUPE SUZANNE LENGLEN
adidas

determined and focused in her play. That was never was more clear than at the 2004 Olympic Games in Athens, Greece.

In the last set of the semifinals, Henin was down 1–5. But in a gritty comeback, Henin rallied to win the set 8–6. She went on to win the gold medal in women's singles.

Few had heard of Maria Sharapova in July 2004. Yet there she was, a 17-year-old facing off against Serena Williams for the Wimbledon title. Sharapova stunned Williams that day, and the focused Russian made a name for herself over the next 10 years with her powerful ground strokes. Before retiring in 2020 due to injuries, Sharapova won five Grand Slam singles titles.

Maria Sharapova made a living on the baseline in her long and successful career.

Throughout the Williams sisters' long careers, they inspired many players, including breakout star Coco Gauff. In 2019, Gauff was one of the youngest players to ever compete at Wimbledon. At 15 years old, she faced her idol, Venus Williams, in her first Grand Slam match.

During the match, Gauff kept a cool head and beat Williams 6–4, 6–4. The first-round upset caused players and fans alike to take note of the rising star. Gauff ended up reaching the fourth round of the tournament before falling to the eventual champion, Simona Halep. Tennis legends including Navratilova have said they expect Gauff to make a mark in the tennis world.

Coco Gauff waves to the Wimbledon spectators after winning a match in 2019.

Barilla

MILESTONES

1924
Helen Mills Moody, nicknamed "Little Miss Poker Face," wins two gold medals at the Olympics.

1951
Althea Gibson becomes the first Black player to win a Grand Slam title.

1973
Billie Jean King beats Bobby Riggs in the "Battle of the Sexes" match to take home $100,000 in prize money.

1976
Margaret Court retires from tennis after winning a record 24 Grand Slam titles.

1988
Steffi Graf wins all four Grand Slam tournaments and an Olympic gold medal in the same year.

2003
Serena Williams wins the Australian Open to become the fifth woman to hold all four Grand Slam titles at the same time.

2018
Naomi Osaka upsets Serena Williams at the US Open to win her first Grand Slam title.

GLOSSARY

break
To win a game in tennis when an opponent is serving.

endurance
The ability to keep doing something for a long time.

match point
A point that can end the match.

straight sets
A match won without losing a set.

tactic
A planned action that is used to achieve a certain goal.

volley
A ball hit before it bounces on the court.

TO LEARN MORE

To learn more about legendary women's tennis players, go to **pressboxbooks.com/AllAccess**. These links are routinely monitored and updated to provide the most current information available.

INDEX